Original title:
Frost on the Pines

Copyright © 2024 Swan Charm
All rights reserved.

Author: Daisy Dewi
ISBN HARDBACK: 978-9908-52-002-5
ISBN PAPERBACK: 978-9908-52-003-2
ISBN EBOOK: 978-9908-52-004-9

The Serene Frostbite

In the stillness of night,
Snowflakes fall like whispers,
Blanketing the world white,
Crystals dance, time lingers.

Branches bow with grace,
A quilt of frozen dreams,
Silent beauty in place,
Nature's gentle schemes.

Icicles softly gleam,
Suspended, fragile, bright,
Reflecting silver beams,
In the soft, pale light.

Footprints tell a story,
Of wanderers who tread,
In this quiet glory,
Where echoes gently spread.

The air, crisp and clear,
Breath visible in the cold,
A moment to revere,
Winter's secret, untold.

Crystal Lattice Overhead

Above, the stars aglow,
Framed by frost's fine lace,
In the night's tranquil flow,
Time finds its sacred space.

Each pattern, each design,
Whispers of winter's art,
Nature's hand, so divine,
Crafts magic in the dark.

Beneath a pale moonlight,
Silence reigns all around,
Holding still the soft night,
Where calm and peace are found.

The world, in slumber deep,
Wrapped in a frosted quilt,
In dreams, we gently leap,
As silent magic builds.

Awake, yet fast asleep,
In each breath, the chill flows,
In this lattice, we keep,
The secrets that winter knows.

A Silent Winter's Tale

Whispers on the wind call,
Echoes through the trees,
As winter's breath enthralls,
Sharing secrets with ease.

Snowflakes weave a story,
Of a land dressed in white,
A timeless, soft glory,
Wrapped in silence so tight.

In the hearth, embers glow,
Warmth in the chill around,
As outside, frost will show,
Nature's beauty unbound.

Each moment lingers long,
In this frozen embrace,
A melody, a song,
Of peace in winter's grace.

The stars above shine bright,
Guardians of the night sky,
As we hold moments tight,
In winter's tender sigh.

In the Grip of the Cold

Frosted breath in the air,
Winter reigns supreme now,
Crystals spark with a glare,
Nature takes a deep bow.

Branches weighed with snow's kiss,
A world stripped bare and clean,
In the chill, there's pure bliss,
Whispers soft and serene.

The ground, a canvas white,
Where footsteps leave their mark,
Underneath the pale light,
A dance in the stark dark.

Embers crackle and glow,
Inside, warmth sort of thrums,
Outside, the cold winds blow,
Winter's rhythm hums.

In this frozen embrace,
Time slows, peace takes its hold,
Each moment leaves a trace,
In the grip of the cold.

Crystal Veil on Evergreen

A crystal veil drapes the trees,
Sparkling jewels catch the breeze.
Nature's breath, a silent sigh,
Underneath the cobalt sky.

Frosted leaves, a glimmering sight,
Whispers of the morning light.
Every branch, a sculpted art,
Cloaked in beauty, nature's heart.

Through the woods, a gentle hush,
In the calm, the senses rush.
Footsteps crunch on frozen ground,
In this peace, lost dreams are found.

Chilling Caress of the Morning

Morning breaks with icy breath,
A chilling caress, whispers of death.
The world adorned in silver lace,
A tranquil scene, a hushed embrace.

Sunrise glimmers on the frost,
Each sparkling jewel, never lost.
Birds awake, their songs are clear,
Echoing the silence near.

Shadows stretch beneath the trees,
A playful dance upon the leaves.
Morning's chill, a fleeting tease,
A fleeting touch upon the breeze.

Nature's Icy Embrace

Nature's breath, a frosty chill,
Whispered secrets, soft and still.
Cold fingers trace the hills in white,
A canvas pure, bathed in light.

Trees stand tall with crowns of ice,
Each branch a mirrored paradise.
Life holds still in crisp embrace,
Time slows down in this quiet space.

Beneath the sky of hazy grey,
Frosted dreams weave night and day.
In every flake that falls from high,
Is nature's love, a gentle sigh.

Silent Shroud of Dawn

Dawn approaches with a muffled sound,
A silent shroud wraps all around.
Soft hues of pink, the world takes flight,
Awakening with the first soft light.

Shadows retreat, their time is done,
The beauty of dawn has just begun.
With every ray, new hopes arise,
Painting dreams across the skies.

In stillness held, the moments sigh,
A breath that lingers, soft goodbye.
As day breaks, we start anew,
In this dawn, a world in view.

Chill Breezes in Evergreen Valleys

Whispers of the trees, so light,
Flowing gently in the night.
Moonlit paths in shadows weave,
Nature's magic, hearts believe.

Crisp air dances, spirits rise,
Underneath the starry skies.
Softly singing through the pines,
Beckoning in quiet lines.

Meadows glisten, dew drops gleam,
Every moment, like a dream.
Footsteps echo, soft and near,
In this realm, there's naught to fear.

Breezes carry tales of old,
Stories in the air unfold.
Life's embrace in every breath,
Rich with meaning, free from death.

In these valleys, time stands still,
Every feeling, every thrill.
With the dawn, the world awakes,
Chill breezes dance, the heart shakes.

Picturesque Scenes of Winter's Hold

Blankets white on hills so wide,
Nature's canvas, pure and bright.
Picturesque, the world adorned,
In winter's grip, we are reborn.

Icicles dangle, crystal clear,
Whispers of the cold draw near.
Snowflakes flutter, soft as air,
Each a wonder, free of care.

Fires crackle, warmth inside,
While outside, chilly winds collide.
Hot cocoa steams beside the glow,
As winter whispers all its woe.

Footprints trail on snowy plains,
Silent journeys, calm remains.
Breathe the chill, embrace the night,
Winter cradles, pure delight.

Seasons change, as they must do,
Yet winter holds its magic true.
Picturesque scenes, forever bold,
In winter's charm, our hearts are sold.

The Hushed Glow of Snowy Pines

Underneath the moon's soft light,
Snowy pines, a wondrous sight.
Silence blankets every sound,
In this beauty, peace is found.

Branches heavy, softly sway,
Whispers of the night at play.
Hushed glow of the frost so bright,
Guides our dreams in gentle flight.

Crystals glitter, stars above,
Nature wrapped in endless love.
Every moment, still and clear,
Echoes of the heart draw near.

Beneath the skies of velvet hue,
Snowy paths invite the new.
Let us wander, hand in hand,
Through the magic of this land.

In the forest, time is lost,
Finding beauty, no matter the cost.
The hushed glow, our hearts entwined,
In snowy pines, peace we find.

Enigma of the Frozen Canopy

Frosted branches, secrets hold,
Mysteries in whispers told.
In the silence, shadows dance,
Enigma waits, a fleeting chance.

Glittering lights in twilight's grasp,
Nature's wonders, we must clasp.
Beneath the boughs, tranquility,
Frozen secrets, softly free.

Silvery breezes twist and twine,
Through the branches, thoughts divine.
Every heartbeat, every sigh,
Echoes softly, asking why.

Journey through this frosted maze,
Finding warmth in winter's gaze.
The canopy above us glows,
As the chill beneath us flows.

In this world where time stands still,
Every moment, ours to fill.
The enigma whispers sweet and low,
In the frozen wonder, we both grow.

Whispers of Crystal Branches

Beneath the frozen sky, they sway,
Their crystal limbs in soft array.
A gentle hush, a snowfall's breath,
In winter's grip, they dance with death.

Whispers ride the frosty air,
Secrets tangled in each snare.
Branches bow with heavy dust,
In the silent night, we trust.

Moonlit shadows weave their light,
Casting dreams in the deep night.
Every glimmer, a story told,
Of magic realms where hearts get bold.

The world beneath, so calm, serene,
In crystal lanes, a silky sheen.
Nature's breath, a soft embrace,
In winter's arms, we find our place.

So let us walk through this delight,
Where whispers rest and spark the night.
For in the glimmering, we shall see,
The crystal branches' mystery.

Enchanted Winter Veil

A blanket white covers the ground,
In silence vast, a peace is found.
Each flake a story, soft and true,
The winter veil, a wondrous view.

Evergreens dressed in frosty lace,
Stand sentinel in time and space.
While frozen streams like glass do flow,
Reflecting stars in twilight's glow.

Footprints trace a tale of glee,
In frosted fields where shadows flee.
With each step, the whispers play,
Of seasons past, now far away.

In swirling twirls, the snowflakes fall,
A dance of nature, a silent call.
Underneath the ethereal light,
The world transforms into pure white.

Beneath this veil, life softly sleeps,
While in our hearts, the magic keeps.
For every snow, a wish is made,
In winter's dreams, our hopes cascade.

Echoes of Icy Silence

In the vastness, a silence reigns,
Where echoes whisper through icy chains.
Among the trees, a stillness posed,
Nature's breath in frost enclosed.

Crystals hang from branches bare,
A frozen world beyond compare.
With every step in soft, white drifts,
We hear the hush, as time shifts.

An owl calls in distant flight,
Breaking the calm of the night.
Frozen ponds, like mirrors shine,
Reflecting dreams, both yours and mine.

Beneath the sky, so deep and wide,
The icy dragons softly glide.
In silence loud and profound,
Life's hidden rhythms can be found.

So let us listen, hearts aligned,
To the echoes of the undefined.
For in this chill, we find our trance,
In icy silence, spirits dance.

The Shimmering Canopy

Above us sways a shimmering sea,
Of icicles and frost so free.
Light cascades through twinkling boughs,
An enchanted realm that softly bows.

The leaves are cloaked in sparkling light,
Magic wrapped in winter's night.
Each branch a wand, each flake a gem,
In nature's night, our diadem.

Beneath this wondrous, twinkling show,
The world transforms, a vibrant glow.
With every step, the starlight sighs,
As night unveils the velvet skies.

Whispers travel on the breeze,
In the canopy, a dance of trees.
Each shimmer casts a spell so rare,
Binding hearts in the winter air.

So let us wander through this light,
Under the stars so bold and bright.
For in the shimmering canopy,
We find our dreams, wild and free.

The Silent Story of the North

In the stillness of the night,
Whispers echo through the trees,
Northern lights dance bright,
Telling tales of ancient seas.

Frosty breath upon the air,
Branches drape in silver sheen,
Nature's secrets laid bare,
In the shadows, peaceful scene.

Snowflakes twirl like fleeting dreams,
Softly landing on the ground,
Crystalline in moonlit beams,
Silence wraps the world around.

Each footprint marks a path anew,
Stories carved in frozen ground,
Beneath a sky so vast and blue,
The north's soft lullaby is found.

So listen close and you may find,
A melody from times of old,
In the quiet, are entwined,
The tales that nature has told.

Winter's Gentle Caress

A soft touch upon the face,
Winter whispers sweet and low,
With each chill, a warm embrace,
In its breath, a silver glow.

Frosted fields in morning light,
The world wears a robe of white,
Nature sleeps yet feels so right,
Beneath the stars, a wondrous sight.

Rivers flow in icy grace,
Singing songs of days gone by,
Every turn, a hidden place,
Where the silent breezes sigh.

Snowflakes dance on winter's air,
A ballet in the chilly breeze,
Glimmers bright without a care,
Crafting magic with such ease.

So let us dream in winter's hold,
Wrapped in warmth, a cozy nest,
Heartfelt stories to be told,
In the quiet, we find rest.

A Hush of Snowy Shadows

Softly falling from above,
Shadows play in snowy light,
Each one whispers of the love,
Held within the winter night.

Footprints lead to secret places,
Wonders hidden deep and wide,
Each step brings new warm embraces,
Where the heart and soul collide.

A blanket white, a calming view,
Stars awake in velvet skies,
Every hush feels fresh and new,
Painting dreams with gentle sighs.

Frosty winds weave stories here,
In the quiet, hear their cheer,
In the shimmer, find the near,
Of snowy shadows, pure and clear.

So linger long where magic flows,
In the chill, the warmth is near,
As a hush of winter glows,
Every moment, crystal clear.

Frost-Kissed Whispers

Morning breaks with glistening light,
Winter cradles all that's bright,
Frost-kissed whispers on the breeze,
Rustling softly through the trees.

Gentle flakes begin to fall,
Drifting down like whispered dreams,
Each one holds a silent call,
In the hush, the spirit beams.

Nature wraps in icy grace,
Blanketing the world in calm,
Every corner finds a space,
To be touched by winter's palm.

Silent nights and starlit skies,
Where the moon lends warmth in glow,
Beneath the vast and silent sighs,
Frost-kissed whispers gently flow.

So embrace this treasured time,
Let the chill invite you near,
In winter's prose, a gentle rhyme,
With each breath, the heart will cheer.

A Bough's Quiet Cry

In the shadow of the trees,
A bough bends with the breeze.
Whispers of a gentle sigh,
Like a longing, quiet cry.

Leaves of green have turned to gray,
As the light begins to fray.
A memory of days gone by,
Echoes in the bough's soft cry.

Frosty breath upon the wood,
Holding secrets, understood.
Time it seems, just drifts away,
Where the bough greets the day.

Underneath the weight of snow,
Silent tales begin to flow.
With each flake a tear set free,
A bough's grief, a mystery.

And as dusk begins to fall,
Nature's song, a solemn call.
In the quiet, hear the sigh,
Of a bough's unspoken cry.

The Beauty of Icy Days

Glistening under winter's light,
Every branch adorned just right.
A world wrapped in silence deep,
Where the dreams of snowflakes sleep.

Brittle air, a crystal hue,
Paints the earth in shades anew.
In the stillness, shadows play,
A ballet of icy display.

Footsteps crunch on frozen ground,
Nature's breath, a tranquil sound.
In the chill, there lies a grace,
Beauty found in every place.

Frozen ponds reflect the night,
Stars above, a twinkling sight.
Under the canopy of gray,
Life endures these icy days.

And though warmth feels far away,
In this cold, hearts learn to sway.
Finding joy in winter's art,
A quiet beauty warms the heart.

Requiem for the Warmth

Fires flicker, shadows loom,
In the cabin's cozy room.
Hearth and heart echo the past,
Memories of warmth amassed.

A requiem for sunlit days,
In the cold, the spirit sways.
Each ember glows, a whisper low,
Of summer's love, a gentle flow.

Outside, the chilling winds do wail,
Through the trees, a haunting tale.
Nature clings to frosty nights,
As the world waits for the light.

Yet in the frost, there's beauty found,
Within the silence, soft and sound.
A delicate dance of frost and flame,
In winter's touch, we find the same.

So we gather, hearts entwined,
In the cold, our warmth aligned.
A toast to warmth, both near and far,
In every shadow, a glowing star.

The Still Dance of Winter Branches

In the quiet, branches sway,
To a rhythm, soft and gray.
Winter's sigh, a gentle beat,
A dance with frost beneath their feet.

Snowflakes tumble, twirl, and glide,
On the boughs, they softly ride.
In stillness, beauty finds its place,
A winter's waltz, a slow embrace.

Branches bow in humble grace,
Painting art in nature's space.
Every movement, calm and light,
In the hush of falling night.

Silent stones beneath the snow,
Witness to the life below.
The still dance that nature shows,
In the cold, the spirit grows.

Listen close, the world in trance,
To the still dance of branches' stance.
Each soft rustle teaches free,
How to find tranquility.

Starlit Frost

In the quiet night, stars gleam,
Softly blanketing earth in chill,
Each breath fogs, like a waking dream,
Nature whispers; the world stands still.

Crystals form on every branch,
The moon dances on frosty floor,
A silvery glow, a soft romance,
Winter's magic forevermore.

Footprints vanish in the white,
Echoes fade into the pines,
The chill brings hearts close, so tight,
Warmth shared, where the silence shines.

Beneath a veil of frost's embrace,
Time slows down, a gentle pause,
In this moment, find your place,
Embrace the beauty, just because.

Through branches bare, the starlight flows,
A tapestry of night's delight,
In starlit frost, the wonder grows,
A silent hymn in winter's night.

Whispers of a North Wind

The north wind sings its haunting song,
Through the trees, it weaves and sways,
Whispers echo, strong yet long,
Carrying tales of ancient days.

Frozen breath of winter's chill,
Crisp and clean as the fall of night,
Over the hills, a quiet thrill,
Guided by the stars so bright.

In the shadows, whispers creep,
Secrets hidden in the cold,
While the world lies fast asleep,
The wind tells stories yet untold.

Each gust brings a gentle nudge,
A reminder of the frozen breath,
Nature's voice, it will not budge,
Echoing softly, beyond death.

Listen closely, heed the call,
Let the north wind fill your soul,
For in its melody, we fall,
Into the night, it makes us whole.

Shadows of a Winter's Night

Shadows dance in candle's glow,
Softly laced in winter's breath,
Every flicker tells us so,
Life persists, defying death.

Silent streets with snowflakes twirl,
Beneath the blanket, warmth remains,
In the chill, a dream unfurls,
Hushed secrets woven in the veins.

Footsteps echo, a distant sound,
Crisp and clear in the stillness found,
In the darkness, joy is crowned,
Winter's magic, around us bounds.

Cold moonlight casts its silver tale,
On frosted windows, love ignites,
In every heart, winter's veil,
Draws us in on shadowed nights.

In these hours, we find our grace,
Wrapped in peace, our spirits rise,
In shadows where we find our place,
Beneath the stars, where the heart lies.

Beneath the Arctic Sky

Beneath the sky, so wide and free,
The Arctic breathes in frigid air,
A world untouched, wild majesty,
Pure beauty, beyond compare.

Endless nights hold whispers true,
Stars like diamonds, bright and bold,
In this realm of white and blue,
Ancient wonders to behold.

Icebergs float in gentle grace,
Carving paths through waters deep,
Nature's artistry, a timeless place,
In the stillness, secrets sleep.

Each wind's gust tells a new tale,
From polar bears to glistening seas,
In the quiet, hear their wail,
As life thrives beneath the freeze.

Together, we share this space,
Under the Arctic's endless glow,
Where every heart finds its embrace,
And beauty dances in the snow.

When the World Turns White

Snowflakes drift on gentle air,
Blanketing the world with care.
Footsteps soft, the silence deep,
In winter's hold, the earth does sleep.

Branches wear a frosty crown,
Peaceful shrouds of white renown.
Nature whispers, calm and still,
While time obeys the winter's will.

Dreams are woven in the chill,
With every flake, the heart is still.
Underneath the quilted skies,
Hope lies buried, waiting to rise.

Candles flicker, shadows play,
In the glow of dusk's soft gray.
The world, transformed, a gleaming sight,
When the world turns pure and white.

The Icy Chorus of the Woods

Echoes of a chilling song,
Whispers weave where winds belong.
Frosted trees in quiet rows,
Guard the secrets winter knows.

Crystals gleam on every bough,
Nature's art, a sacred vow.
Moonlight dances through the leaves,
Enchanting dreams that winter weaves.

Silent sentinels stand tall,
Listening to the winter's call.
With each note, a breath departs,
In harmony, the forest's heart.

Snowy blankets hug the ground,
In their cradle, peace is found.
Underneath the soft, white veil,
The icy chorus starts to sail.

A Dance of Shivering Pines

Pines sway gently to the breeze,
Whispers soft among the trees.
Snowflakes whisper in their dance,
Nature twirls, a snowy trance.

Branches bend and bow with grace,
Embracing winter's cold embrace.
Under stars, the night unfolds,
Stories written, yet untold.

Frosty breaths in chilly air,
Breathe in magic everywhere.
With each step, the forest hums,
A rhythm that forever comes.

Draped in white, the world stands still,
In the silence, hear the thrill.
As shadow dances in moonlight,
A dance of shivering pine takes flight.

Crystalline Murmurs of the Forest

In forest depths, the crystals gleam,
A language wrought from winter's dream.
Beneath the frost, a sparkling glow,
Nature's art in silence flows.

Murmurs echo, soft and pure,
Binding all with threads demure.
Branches whisper tales of yore,
In the stillness, spirits soar.

Each step taken, snowflakes sigh,
As hidden wonders drift by.
A frozen stream, a silent press,
Captures time in winter's dress.

Where shadows lay, and light is few,
Crystalline visions come in view.
A tapestry of white unfolds,
In murmurs soft, the forest holds.

A Tapestry of Frozen Needles

In the stillness of the night,
Snowflakes fall like whispered dreams.
They weave a blanket, pure and white,
A tapestry of frozen beams.

Pines stand tall against the sky,
Adorned in nature's glistening dress.
Beneath their boughs, the silence lies,
In tranquil beauty, we find our rest.

Crystals shimmer in the moon's glow,
A dance of cold upon the land.
Each step we take, a soft echo,
A fleeting touch, a gentle hand.

Time stands still in this wonder,
Magic lingers in the air.
The world is hushed, free from thunder,
An embrace of peace, pure and rare.

As dawn breaks, the light reclaims,
The colors shift, the shadows fade.
Yet in our hearts, the memory remains,
Of frozen needles, nature's serenade.

Twilight's Chilled Embrace

Beneath the canopy of stars,
Twilight whispers secrets low.
The world transforms, as night imparts,
A chilly breath, a gentle flow.

Frosty air wraps close and tight,
The whispers of the ancient trees.
In twilight's arms, the soft moonlight,
Calls to the heart with soothing ease.

Crisp leaves crunch beneath our feet,
Echoes of a day well spent.
While shadows gather, shadows meet,
Where dreams, like stars, are gently sent.

The night unfolds, a velvet hue,
With every breeze, a painter's stroke.
In this calm, love feels anew,
As winter's hand begins to cloak.

With every moment, time stands still,
Lost in the magic of the night.
In twilight's chilled embrace, we will,
Find solace in the soft moonlight.

Beneath the Silver-Lined Boughs

Among the branches, soft and low,
Silver linings catch the eye.
Whispers of secrets start to flow,
In the cool shadows where dreams lie.

The world below rests, deep asleep,
While stars above begin to shine.
Under these boughs, our hearts will keep,
Moments that feel like the divine.

Light dances through the leaves of green,
Painting patterns soft and bright.
Here in the calm, we're ever keen,
To savor hours spun with light.

Frost-kissed air creates a song,
Nature's choir, pure and sweet.
Around us, echoes softly throng,
As pathways meet beneath our feet.

The night holds promises untold,
In whispers wrapped in silver thread.
Beneath the boughs, our dreams unfold,
In tender sighs, where love is bred.

Glimmers on Evergreen Dreams

Amidst the gloom, a spark appears,
Glimmers dance on evergreen dreams.
With subtle light, they wipe our fears,
A tapestry of hope that beams.

Pinecone whispers share the night,
While shadows play in golden beams.
Each moment lingers, pure delight,
In the soft tune of distant streams.

Fragrant earth beneath our feet,
A cradle for the calm and still.
Here, nature gifts a warm retreat,
In quiet beauty, hearts we fill.

Stars emerge from their cozy naps,
Guiding lost wanderers with ease.
In these woods, we map our paths,
To find our peace among the trees.

As dawn arrives, the colors swell,
With glimmers bright, the world awakes.
In evergreen, our hearts will dwell,
For every moment, joy creates.

Glimmering Needles Under Moonlight

Glimmers dance on needles bright,
In the calm of silver night.
Whispers soft, the shadows play,
Guiding dreams until the day.

In the air, a fragrant pine,
Nature's secrets intertwine.
Silent paths where my heart roams,
Under starlit forest domes.

Moonbeams trace the forest floor,
Softly calling, wanting more.
Each breath taken, crisp and clear,
Lost in beauty, free from fear.

Glistening dew on every leaf,
Each moment pure, beyond belief.
Carried by the gentle breeze,
Wrapped in night's sweet memories.

Time slips by, yet still I stand,
In this magical, serene land.
Underneath the lunar glow,
Where the glimmering wonders flow.

Shimmering Silence of the Woods

In the woods, a hush so deep,
Where the ancient shadows sleep.
Leaves will whisper tales untold,
In a language soft and bold.

Branches arch in graceful flight,
Framing dreams in fading light.
Every step, a sacred sound,
In this stillness, peace is found.

Misty breaths, the air so sweet,
Nature's pulse, a gentle beat.
Sunlight plays on emerald blades,
Dancing lightly in the glades.

Here I pause, my spirit soars,
In the silence, nature roars.
Heartbeats echo, time stands still,
As the woods fulfill my will.

Through the trees, a pathway calls,
Guided by the night's soft thralls.
Embraced in stillness, I will roam,
In the woods, I find my home.

Winter's Breath on Boughs

Winter's breath on boughs does cling,
Transforming woods into a king.
Frosted tips in morning light,
Shimmer softly, pure and white.

Crystals form on every tree,
Nature's touch, a sight to see.
Every branch adorned with care,
Weaving magic through the air.

Snowflakes dance, a swirling tide,
In the silence, dreams abide.
Hushed and still, the world asleep,
As the night begins to creep.

Beneath blankets soft and deep,
Nature cradles those who weep.
In the chill, there lies a grace,
Embraced in winter's warm embrace.

As the moonlight bathes the land,
I can feel the softest hand.
Guiding me through snow and frost,
In this beauty, never lost.

Frosted Dreams In Twilight

Twilight falls, the world aglow,
Frosted dreams in soft winds blow.
Lavender skies turn shades of grey,
As the sun begins to sway.

Dew-kissed grass, a shimmering view,
Reflecting colors, bright and true.
In this moment, time stands still,
Wrapped in twilight's gentle thrill.

Whispers float on evening air,
Carried softly, without care.
The stars awaken one by one,
As the day is finally done.

Night unfolds with velvet grace,
Drawing shadows on my face.
All the world begins to sleep,
In this beauty oh so deep.

Frosted dreams, a fleeting sight,
In the hush of coming night.
I will cherish moments few,
Lost in twilight's sweet adieu.

Icy Tapestries in the Woodlands

In the quiet woods they gleam,
Their beauty catching every beam.
Delicate threads of frosty lace,
Weaving magic, a hidden space.

Beneath the boughs, the silence reigns,
While nature softly breaks the chains.
Branches hold the jeweled dew,
A wonderland crafted anew.

Footprints crunch on the snowy ground,
Whispers of winter all around.
Each step taken, a gentle sigh,
Beneath the vast and azure sky.

Frost-kissed leaves in sunlight dance,
Inviting us to pause, to glance.
In icy tapestries, dreams unfold,
A quiet tale in silver and gold.

As dusk descends, the shadows grow,
A tapestry hidden at twilight's glow.
In the woodlands, our hearts align,
With the icy beauty, pure, divine.

Winter's Canvas of Light and Shade

A canvas stretched on winter's breath,
Where light and shade dance close to death.
Brushstrokes of frost paint every tree,
In a world wrapped in serenity.

The sun peeks through with hesitant grace,
Illuminating nature's hidden face.
Shadows creep and gently sway,
Winter whispers in soft relay.

Frozen streams mirror the skies,
Reflecting clouds like distant cries.
Each branch heavy with icy weights,
A world adorned with nature's traits.

In this silence, magic thrives,
Breathing life to dormant lives.
Winter's canvas, both bold and bright,
Captivating hearts in its soft light.

As twilight falls, colors blend,
Where day meets night, they softly mend.
A masterpiece of white and grey,
Winter holds its breath, a grand display.

Shards of Ice in the Morning Glow

Morning breaks with a gentle sigh,
Sunlight glimmers, paints the sky.
Shards of ice on branches gleam,
As if awakened from a dream.

The air is crisp, a breath so rare,
Each crystal sparkling, beyond compare.
With every step, the world does crack,
Whispers of winter on the track.

The horizon blushes with soft light,
Turning the dark into a sight.
Shards of ice reflect the dawn,
A fleeting beauty, gently drawn.

Nature's palette, fresh and new,
Bathed in colors, deep and true.
In each moment, a story told,
In magic shards, the winter's gold.

As the day unfolds its wings,
In every corner, beauty sings.
These shards of ice, a fleeting show,
In morning's glow, we're free to flow.

Resplendent Branches at Dusk

As day retreats, the colors blend,
In a tapestry where shadows mend.
Resplendent branches, kissed by night,
Wrap the world in soft twilight.

The horizon burns with crimson flames,
Painting the sky with nature's claims.
Each branch adorned, a work of art,
Whispering secrets of the heart.

Stars begin to twinkle bright,
In the embrace of the coming night.
Resplendent branches, bold and tall,
Stand as sentinels, guarding all.

Cool breezes whisper through the trees,
Carrying tales on the gentle breeze.
In dusk's embrace, we find our peace,
Preparing for night's soft release.

In the silence, dreams take flight,
As shadows deepen, banishing light.
Resplendent branches hold us near,
In the quiet dark, we've naught to fear.

The Captivating Hush Beneath

In shadows deep the whispers sigh,
The earth holds secrets, low and shy.
A gentle breeze, it sweeps the ground,
A tranquil peace in silence found.

The leaves are still, the branches bare,
An unseen pulse, a tender care.
Beneath the frost, life stirs awake,
In quietude, each breath we take.

The softest touch of winter's hand,
Caresses all across the land.
A captivating hush unfolds,
In nature's heart, the warmth still holds.

With every flake that falls from skies,
The world transforms, a grand disguise.
In this stillness, dreams take flight,
A tapestry of day and night.

So linger here, amidst the calm,
Feel the pulse, the quiet balm.
For in this hush, the spirit flows,
A boundless peace that nature knows.

Whirling Leaves in Winter's Chill

The autumn winds begin to wane,
As winter's breath brings forth the rain.
Whirling leaves take flight and glide,
In swirling dance, they drift and slide.

With colors bold, they bid goodbye,
A fleeting grace beneath the sky.
They sparkle bright, a fleeting song,
In nature's realm where they belong.

As temperatures drop, the chill sets in,
The world transforms, a new begin.
Whirling leaves in the frosty air,
Embrace the cold with vibrant flair.

Each gust of wind, a playful tease,
Among the branches, through the trees.
They twist and spin, a wild ballet,
In winter's grasp, they dance and sway.

While silence reigns, the beauty gleams,
In frosted light, we catch our dreams.
For whirling leaves in winter's chill,
Remind us all to pause, be still.

A Wintry Tale of Nature's Grace

In the whisper of the pines, so tall,
A wintry tale begins to call.
The fields are draped in glistening white,
Where starlit skies embrace the night.

With every flake, a story spun,
Of fleeting days and ancient sun.
Nature's brush paints all it sees,
In gentle strokes upon the breeze.

The footprints left, a fleeting trace,
In nature's dance, we find our place.
Each breath of air, a tale retold,
Of warmth amidst the winter cold.

As icicles hang from rooftops bold,
The world awaits, a sight to behold.
A wintry tale, so pure and bright,
In every corner, sparkles light.

So hold this moment, stay awhile,
In winter's charm, embrace the smile.
For nature's grace in frozen streams,
Reflects the life within our dreams.

Ethereal Dance of Snow and Silence

In twilight's glow, the world transforms,
As snowflakes fall in graceful swarms.
An ethereal dance, so soft, so slow,
Whispers of beauty where silence flows.

Each flake a wish from skies above,
A gentle touch, a sign of love.
They twirl and spin, a swirling sea,
In winter's arms, we long to be.

With every hush that blankets ground,
A symphony of peace is found.
Among the trees, like dreams in flight,
A silent world bathed in silver light.

As night descends, a cloak of dreams,
The moonlit glow on frozen streams.
Each breath of air, a moment's grace,
In nature's realm, we find our place.

So let us dance in snow's embrace,
And cherish every fleeting trace.
For in this stillness, hearts align,
In ethereal beauty, pure and fine.

Luminous Shadows on the Trail

Whispers dance in evening's glow,
Shadows stretch where soft winds blow.
Footprints echo on the ground,
Stories linger all around.

Moonlight weaves through ancient trees,
Guiding dreamers with its ease.
Stars awaken, twinkling bright,
Illuminating the night.

Creatures stir in silent grace,
Finding comfort in this space.
Every rustle, every sound,
Nature's secrets to be found.

Paths entwine like lovers' sighs,
Beneath a tapestry of skies.
With each step, a new delight,
Drawn by shadows, lost in light.

So tread softly on this trail,
Where luminous dreams shall prevail.
Let your heart be free and wild,
In nature's arms, forever a child.

Unveiling the Crystal Boughs

In the hush of morning light,
Crystal boughs gleam pure and bright.
Nature's jewels, softly spun,
Catch the rays of waking sun.

Branches draped in icy lace,
Every glimmer holds a grace.
Whispers of the frost's soft hand,
Transforming every speck of land.

Beneath this canopy of frost,
Life and warmth will never be lost.
Each twig cradles winter's breath,
A testament to life and death.

Birds take flight, a fleeting sight,
Through the frost, they seek the light.
Songs of joy begin to rise,
Among the sparkles in the skies.

Thus the boughs, in stillness, show,
A world of beauty cloaked in snow.
And as the sun begins to climb,
The crystal boughs weave dreams in time.

A Frosty Portrait of the Woods

Canvas white, the world transformed,
In winter's chill, the silence warmed.
Every branch a work of art,
Frosty fingers, nature's heart.

Footsteps crunch on frozen ground,
Echoes in the air abound.
Trees stand tall, like sentinels,
Guarding secrets, ancient spells.

Frozen streams reflect the sky,
Carrying whispers on the fly.
Nature paints in hues of gray,
Each shadow deepens with the day.

Sunlight peeks through scattered leaves,
Shattering frost, as nature grieves.
Yet life stirs beneath the white,
Awakening in soft twilight.

A portrait drawn of peace profound,
In every corner, magic found.
The woods, alive with frosty tales,
In winter's grasp, the spirit sails.

Serenity in Icy Encounter

Quiet falls as snowflakes weave,
A tapestry where souls believe.
In this stillness lies a balm,
Embracing hearts, a soothing calm.

Breath of winter, crisp and clear,
Every moment held so dear.
Underneath the icy breath,
Lies a promise, staving death.

Trees adorned in frosted white,
Glimmer softly, pure delight.
Whispers travel on the breeze,
Carrying tales from ancient trees.

In icy chambers, thoughts align,
A dance of beauty, pure and fine.
Each flake a story, each sigh a tune,
In the embrace of winter's moon.

Here, serenity finds its place,
In every shard of frozen grace.
A moment held, forever true,
In icy encounter, me and you.

A Dance of Ice and Shadows

In the moonlight, whispers sway,
Silent figures glide and play.
Frosted winds weave through the air,
Echoes of a world laid bare.

Shadowed faces, gleaming bright,
Twinkling stars, a dazzling sight.
Footsteps hush on winter's breath,
A waltz of life embraced by death.

Glistening paths of silver hue,
Mysteries cold, yet all so true.
Frozen dreams and secrets speak,
In the darkness, emotions peak.

Whirling dancers, graceful, free,
Chilled by the night's reverie.
Nature's rhythm, sharp and clear,
Echoes of the heart we hear.

As the dawn begins to break,
Ice and shadows start to shake.
Fleeting moments, time will show,
A dance that only cold winds know.

Nurtured by the Cold

Underneath the heavy frost,
Life awakens, never lost.
Silent blankets, soft and deep,
Secrets in the snow we keep.

Branches bend with crystal weight,
Nature's breath, a tranquil state.
Shapes in white, a canvas pure,
Hope and peace, we must endure.

Through the chill, new dreams arise,
Pale sunbeams paint the skies.
Winter's touch, a tender hand,
Guiding souls across the land.

Every flake a story told,
Written in the veins of cold.
Wrapped in silence, warm embrace,
In the cold, we find our place.

Seeds of beauty, frozen tight,
Waiting for the spring's daylight.
Nurtured by the cold, they thrive,
In winter's heart, we feel alive.

The Quiet Thaw of Night

Stars above begin to fade,
Underneath, the world remade.
Gentle whispers, soft and light,
Wrapping all in velvet night.

Ice that melts in subtle ways,
Lengthening of vibrant days.
Creaking branches, sighs of trees,
Brought to life by warming breeze.

Echoes linger, past still clear,
Memory of winter near.
Nature's palette shifts and sways,
Colors springing from the grays.

As the shadows stretch and bend,
Quietly the seasons blend.
In the stillness, we can find,
Beauty woven, intertwined.

Night will yield and slowly fade,
Promises of warmth displayed.
In each moment, life will flow,
Gentle, sweet, the quiet thaw.

Enchanted by the Chill

Glistening frost upon the leaves,
Magic whispers through the eves.
Every breath, a spark ignites,
In the chill of winter nights.

Fairy tales in shadows weave,
Nature's song, we dare believe.
Icicles like diamond thread,
Crafting stories, gently spread.

Frozen laughter fills the air,
Heartfelt moments, bold and rare.
In the stillness, wonder grows,
A world of dreams where magic flows.

Snowflakes dance, a waltzing cheer,
Painting love in crystal spheres.
In the silence, spirits soar,
Embracing chill forevermore.

Enchanted paths, we tread with care,
Finding peace in winter's glare.
Through the cold, our hearts unite,
In solitude, we find delight.

Nature's Frozen Artistry

The trees wear coats of crystal white,
Their branches dance, a dazzling sight.
In silence deep, the world is still,
A canvas formed by winter's chill.

The rivers flow in icy chains,
Their whispers lost in frosty plains.
Soft snowflakes fall like gentle dreams,
A fleeting touch of nature's schemes.

The mountains stand with heads held high,
They pierce the slate-gray winter sky.
With every breath, the air is pure,
A frosty kiss that's wide and sure.

Beneath the blanket, life hides low,
Awaiting sun and thawing flow.
Yet in this cold, we find our peace,
As nature's art will never cease.

In every flake, a story glows,
Of ancient times and how she grows.
A winter's night, so calm, so bright,
Holds secrets wrapped in purest white.

The Chill of Solitude

In quiet woods, the shadows creep,
Where whispers linger, secrets keep.
The only sound, a distant sigh,
As winter's breath drifts softly by.

Alone beneath the starry dome,
I find a place I can call home.
The chilling air, a friend so near,
In solitude, I lose my fear.

The frost-kissed ground, a carpet fair,
Invites my thoughts to linger there.
With every beat, my heart aligns,
With nature's still, unspoken signs.

Time stands still in this frozen world,
As silent snowflakes gently twirled.
The solitude, a balm-like grace,
In winter's cold, I find my place.

With every breath, a truth unfolds,
The warmth within defies the cold.
Embrace the stillness, let it be,
For in this chill, I am truly free.

Echoes Amidst the Snow

The land lies wrapped in a blanket white,
Where echoes of laughter fade from sight.
Ghostly whispers roam the paths untrod,
In the silence of winter, where peace is God.

Footprints linger, then vanish fast,
Memories fading, shadows cast.
The world holds its breath as snowflakes fall,
Each flake a tale, a soft-spoken call.

In the forest deep, the stillness reigns,
A melody born in frozen veins.
The wind carries secrets from far and wide,
In the heart of winter, they softly bide.

As twilight descends, a hush of awe,
Transforms the landscape, a wonder to draw.
Each echo a memory, echoing clear,
In the arms of the snow, I hold them near.

Yet in this quiet, life waits and sleeps,
While winter's promise silently keeps.
Before the thaw, before the bloom,
Echoes of warmth linger in the gloom.

A Tundra's Embrace

In the stillness of the tundra wide,
Where icy winds and whispers bide.
Beneath the heavens, vast and clear,
I feel the wildness drawing near.

A tapestry of white and gray,
Stitched with shadows, night and day.
Each snowdrift tells a story old,
Of nature's heart, fierce and bold.

The horizon stretches, flat and wide,
A realm where dreams and silence glide.
In every breath, the cold looms near,
Yet warmth within empowers fear.

With every step, the earth unfolds,
A magic ancient, fierce, and bold.
In this embrace of frost and flake,
A bond with nature, none can break.

I close my eyes and feel the grace,
Of gentle snows in winter's embrace.
In the tundra's arms, I find my way,
A part of this wild, frozen ballet.

Glacial Whispers Amongst the Trees

In the stillness, whispers breathe,
Snowflakes dance on chilled exhale.
Branches bow with icy wreaths,
Nature's silence holds a tale.

Moonlight glimmers on the snow,
Shadows flicker, softly sway.
Cool winds carry tales of old,
Of dreams that linger, fade away.

Tranquil echoes in the night,
Murmurs of the ancient wood.
Each layer bathed in silver light,
A world where time is understood.

Amidst the frost, a gentle sigh,
Melodies of winter's grace.
Underneath the endless sky,
Whispers hide in every place.

As dawn breaks with golden hue,
The trees awake, the calm departs.
Yet the glacial whispers too,
Remain within our fragile hearts.

A Touch of Elegance in December

Snowflakes fall like whispered dreams,
Each one unique, a fleeting grace.
The world transformed in silver streams,
A soft embrace, a tender space.

Branches dressed in purest white,
Glisten bright with morning dew.
Every corner, pure delight,
Nature's art in every view.

Candlelight flickers, warmth inside,
Homes adorned in festive cheer.
A symphony of love and pride,
Echoes gently, drawing near.

Children laugh beneath the trees,
Building dreams of snowmen tall.
In the air, a cool, sweet breeze,
December's magic enfolds us all.

As evening falls, the stars appear,
A blanket soft, the sky so wide.
In this moment, love is near,
A touch of elegance, our guide.

Hidden Secrets Beneath Frost

Underneath a blanket white,
Lies a world, asleep but bright.
Memories wrapped in frozen haze,
Awaiting time's warm, tender gaze.

In the crispness of the air,
Whispers linger, secrets share.
Nature holds its breath in peace,
Quiet waits, a soft release.

Every flake a story told,
Of summer's bloom now dreams of cold.
Yet beneath this icy shell,
Life awaits, a secret swell.

Roots entwined in silent prayer,
Yearning for the sun's warm glare.
Patience held in frozen grip,
Waiting for the spring's soft sip.

As sunbeams touch the morning ground,
Hidden life begins to sound.
Frost will yield, and secrets thrive,
In warmth's embrace, the past's alive.

Shadows Dressed in Crystal

Shadows play in winter's light,
Draped in layers, crystal clear.
Branches spark, a beautiful sight,
Nature's canvas, calm and near.

Echoes of the past reside,
In each gleaming facet bright.
A world where secrets softly bide,
Bathed in hues of gentle white.

Steps are muffled, whispers low,
As we wander through the cold.
Every heartbeat, pulse of snow,
Stories wrapped in crystal gold.

Frosted paths lead dreams away,
To places where shadows dance.
In the twilight, spirits sway,
Awakening our hearts to chance.

As night falls, the stars ignite,
Casting dreams on winter's breath.
In shadows dressed in crystal light,
We find beauty in the depth.

Echoes in a Frozen Glade

Whispers dance on icy air,
Footsteps crunch in frosty prayer.
The trees stand silent, tall, and stark,
Echoes linger in the dark.

Moonlight spills like silver dreams,
Chilling night with soft moonbeams.
Nature holds its breath in grace,
In this glade, time finds its place.

Shadows play on fallen snow,
Each flake tells tales of long ago.
Ghostly figures drift and glide,
In this world where wonders hide.

Frosty branches crack and sway,
As the night gives birth to day.
With each heartbeat, silence grows,
In the glade where magic flows.

So let the echoes softly sing,
Of the peace that winter brings.
In frozen lands where dreams align,
We find our hearts, serene, divine.

Luminescent Branches at Dusk

As daylight bows to evening's call,
Branches shimmer, shadows fall.
Colors blend in twilight's paint,
Nature's art, both wild and quaint.

Beneath the sky's soft violet hue,
Leaves glow with a mystic dew.
Each whispering breeze carries light,
Enchanted moments fade from sight.

Stars awaken, one by one,
Glimmers spark like dreams begun.
The forest breathes in tranquil ease,
As twilight kisses ancient trees.

Misty trails weave in and out,
Hints of magic, swirling about.
Every branch a story holds,
In twilight's realm where time unfolds.

Secrets linger in the air,
Woven softly, light and care.
Beneath the twilight's gentle clasp,
In luminescence, we all gasp.

Glacial Kisses on Evergreen

Snowflakes fall like whispered dreams,
Draping trees in silver seams.
Evergreen stands proud and tall,
Cloaked in winter's frozen thrall.

Each bough adorned with icy lace,
Nature's beauty, pure and grace.
The chill caresses all it sees,
In this land of ancient trees.

A soft hush blankets every glade,
As moonlight winks, a gentle shade.
In shadows deep, the stillness flows,
With glacial kisses, love bestows.

Night enfolds with quiet power,
Each moment savored, sweet as flower.
Beneath the stars, dreams take flight,
In the embrace of winter's night.

Echoes of the past remain,
In every flake, a memory's gain.
Glacial magic, soft and clear,
Holds the essence of winter near.

The Chill of Solstice Nights

A frosty breath upon the ground,
In the stillness, peace is found.
Solstice nights, so dark and deep,
While the world around us sleeps.

Stars shine bright in velvet skies,
Holding dreams and ancient sighs.
The air is crisp, the earth is light,
In this calm, the heart takes flight.

Crickets whisper secrets clear,
As the moon draws ever near.
Night unfolds her cloak so wide,
In quiet beauty, souls abide.

Fires crackle, warmth bestowed,
Within our hearts, a gentle code.
Gathered close, we share our tales,
While outside, winter softly exhales.

Nature pauses, takes a breath,
Celebrating life's sweet heft.
In the chill, a promise waits,
For dawn to break and love to sate.

And so we weave the night with light,
Holding close our hopes so bright.
In solstice's embrace, we find,
The treasures of the heart and mind.

Beneath the Weight of Winter

Snowflakes drift in silent dance,
Blanketing the earth's expanse.
Icicles hang like crystal tears,
Whispering secrets of past years.

Branches bow with heavy grace,
Nature draped in white embrace.
Chilled winds hum a muted song,
As winter's night stretches long.

Frosted windows frame the glow,
Of hearths that warm despite the snow.
Footprints crunch on velvet white,
A fleeting trace of life in sight.

Stars concealed by clouds so thick,
Nature's pulse slows to a trick.
In this stillness, time stands still,
Heartbeats echo, soft yet shrill.

Beneath the weight, we find our peace,
In winter's depth, our worries cease.
Embracing all that nature weaves,
Beneath the snow, the world believes.

Ghosts of the Greenwood

Whispers roam through ancient trees,
Echoes carried on the breeze.
Stories linger in the night,
Ghostly forms in silver light.

Mossy roots hold memories close,
Fallen leaves, a soft morose.
Moonlit paths weave threads of lore,
Secrets kept from days of yore.

Faint laughter dances on the air,
Shadows move with a dreamlike flair.
Enchantments whisper from the ferns,
With every gust, the magic churns.

A fantasy where spirits blend,
Every oak a timeless friend.
Underneath the starry spread,
The ghosts of green, forever tread.

In twilight's glow, they softly sway,
Guiding souls who've lost their way.
The woodland's heart beats wild and free,
Forever bound, we all shall be.

The Frozen Symphony

Nature hums a chilly tune,
Underneath the silver moon.
Icicles like crystalline notes,
Frosty breath on winter's coats.

Treetops sway in quiet grace,
While snowflakes dance, a soft embrace.
Each flake a note, unique and bright,
Creating music in the night.

Crickets hush, their song deferred,
The world sleeps on, without a word.
A symphony of silence grows,
As winter's magic softly flows.

Echoes of a world beneath,
Lurking there, a frozen wreath.
In every breath, the chill we share,
Notes of life still linger there.

Within this frozen, raptured scene,
Silent dreams unfold between.
In harmony, we find our way,
The frozen symphony holds sway.

Subtle Beauty in White

The world wears a delicate shroud,
In icy silence, soft and proud.
Blankets of snow, a canvas pure,
Subtle beauty that's ever sure.

Every flake uniquely spun,
Catching light, reflecting fun.
Winter's touch, both cold and kind,
A hidden magic for us to find.

Branches dressed in crystal lace,
Nature's elegance, a timeless grace.
In the quiet, we hear the call,
Of gentle whispers that enthrall.

The softest sigh of twilight's peace,
As day and night begin to cease.
In this stillness, hearts align,
With nature's wonders, pure, divine.

Through frostbit whispers and soft glow,
We see the beauty in the snow.
In white we find our spirits lift,
A subtle beauty, nature's gift.

Glades of Winter's Wonder

In quiet glades where silence reigns,
The frost adorns the bending lanes.
Soft whispers dance on icy ground,
As nature holds her breath, profound.

Beneath the boughs, a carpet white,
Embracing stillness, pure and bright.
The world takes pause, a gentle sigh,
As flurries fall from twilight sky.

A crystal touch on every tree,
The winter's song, a memory.
With every flake a tale untold,
In glades of beauty, soft and cold.

The sunlight glimmers, faint and shy,
Painting hues on high, oh my!
A moment caught in chilly air,
In winter's glades, beyond compare.

So let us wander, hand in hand,
Through frozen paths in wonderland.
In glades of winter, dreams take flight,
Where time stands still in pure delight.

Shards of Light Between the Boughs

In forest deep where shadows play,
The sunbeams find their boldest way.
Through gaps in leaves, they pierce the gloom,
Creating magic, bright as bloom.

A sprinkle of gold on mossy floor,
Awakens life and opens doors.
With every ray, a story spins,
Of whispered secrets, where love begins.

The branches sway, a tender dance,
As light ignites a fleeting chance.
In Nature's arms, the world's alive,
In shards of light, our hearts will thrive.

Beneath the canopy, we seek,
Moments rare and truths we speak.
In soft embrace of dappled sun,
We find our peace, as dreamers run.

So linger here, let time unwind,
In sparkling light, our souls entwined.
A symphony of joy and grace,
In boughs entwined, we find our place.

A Stillness Wrapped in White

The world transformed, a canvas bright,
In stillness wrapped, a purest white.
Each breath is hushed, each heart is still,
As winter weaves her tranquil will.

The trees stand tall, their branches bare,
Adorning white with quiet care.
A magic cloak upon the earth,
Each flake a promise, a sacred birth.

In frosted air, the whispers freeze,
Echoes lost in the gentle breeze.
A moment held, a fleeting grace,
In winter's hush, we find our place.

Though time may pass and seasons change,
This stillness feels both new and strange.
The world sleeps on, a sacred night,
In dreams of snow, we take our flight.

So cherish now this quiet song,
In winter's arms, we all belong.
For in this stillness, hearts unite,
A bond of warmth wrapped in pure white.

Seasonal Secrets Beneath the Trees

The forest breathes with stories deep,
Of whispered secrets, night doesn't keep.
Beneath the boughs, a world unfolds,
In every rustle, life's tales told.

The leaves may dance, the shadows long,
In every sound, a hidden song.
With gentle steps, we wander slow,
In earthy scents, the magic grows.

The roots embrace the world below,
In silent strength, their wisdom flows.
Within the soil, the past remains,
A tapestry of joys and pains.

In twilight's grasp, we stop to see,
The beauty wrapped in mystery.
A harmony in nature's art,
Seasonal secrets touch the heart.

So let us gather by these trees,
To share our hopes upon the breeze.
In nature's arms, we find release,
Seasonal secrets, love and peace.

Lament of the Frozen Pines

The pines stand still, draped in white,
Whispers of sorrow fill the night.
Branches heavy with icy tears,
Nature mourns through endless years.

Brittle winds hum a haunting tune,
Beneath the grey, a hidden moon.
In winter's grasp, they shiver low,
Echoes of life in the frost below.

Frozen shadows dance in silence,
Time itself ceases to make sense.
Yet in their hearts, a warmth remains,
Yearning for spring to break their chains.

Roots buried deep in frozen ground,
Whispers of hope in stillness found.
Awaiting sun to melt the pain,
Eager to rise and bloom again.

Through the chill, a promise gleams,
Life will return with the warmer beams.
Oh, frozen pines, your burden shared,
Life's cycle continues, forever paired.

Whispers Beneath the Snow

Softly the snow blankets the ground,
A hush descends, no other sound.
Beneath the frost, life stirs and sighs,
Murmurs of spring in hidden guise.

Each flake a whisper, secrets spun,
In winter's grasp, the dance's begun.
Roots dream of warmth, of sunlit beams,
While icy sheets cover ancient dreams.

The world in white, a canvas pure,
Nature's quiet, a gentle cure.
Promise of thaw in the days ahead,
As flowers awaken from their bed.

Time crawls slowly in winter's hold,
Yet life awaits, brave and bold.
Beneath the snow, a tale unfolds,
Of warmth and light in the future told.

So let the snow fall, let it embrace,
The earth that soon will find its place.
In whispers soft, spring will arise,
A symphony of life beneath the skies.

Veil of Ice

A curtain hangs of crystal clear,
A fragile shield, both bright and sheer.
Through the veil, the world looks strange,
Each shape and form begins to change.

Icicles dangling, sharp as knives,
Holding secrets of winter lives.
Frost-kissed branches, a dazzling sight,
Trapping moments in the quiet light.

Underneath the frozen glaze,
A whisper stirs in the icy haze.
Life pulses on, though still and shy,
Waiting to break when the thaw draws nigh.

The sun peeks through with warming grace,
A promise made to stir the space.
This veil of ice will soon dissolve,
Allowing life's wild dance to evolve.

Breathe in the chill, embrace the sight,
Nature's beauty, a pure delight.
Through icy dreams, new stories grow,
In the fleeting moments 'neath the snow.

Tree of Dreams

Once a sapling, small and bright,
Reaching upward, kissed by light.
Winds would cradle every sigh,
Nature's whispers, low and high.

Through seasons change, it stood so tall,
Standing firm against the fall.
Leaves like pages, stories spun,
In every gust, a life begun.

Roots entwined with the earth's embrace,
Holding dreams in their sacred space.
Branches echo laughter, fears,
Softly holding all its years.

Under stars, it dreams anew,
Of sunlit paths and skies of blue.
Each ring a memory carved in time,
In silent strength, a steady climb.

The tree of dreams, steadfast and wise,
A witness to the passing skies.
And when it's time to fade away,
Its spirit lives in hearts that stay.

Silvery Hues at Daybreak

Morning breaks with pale light's song,
Chasing shadows where they belong.
Frosted whispers fill the air,
A promise made, beyond compare.

Glistening dew on blades of grass,
Each droplet shines as moments pass.
Soft rays spill on the waking ground,
Nature's brushstrokes, beauty unbound.

Birds begin their morning cry,
Songs of joy that leap and fly.
As colors spread, the world ignites,
A canvas painted with pure delights.

With silvery hues brushing the dawn,
A gentle reminder of life reborn.
Embrace the chill, welcome the light,
For every dusk brings a new delight.

In the quiet of day's first breath,
Whispers of hope that conquer death.
With each new dawn, a chance to see,
The magic alive in you and me.

Nature's Winter Lace

Snowflakes dance on the whispering breeze,
A blanket of white on the slumbering trees.
Each branch adorned with a shimmering sheen,
Nature wrapped up in a quiet routine.

The world holds its breath in a frosty embrace,
Footprints are etched on this soft, gentle lace.
Silence envelops the land deep in night,
While stars twinkle brightly, a beautiful sight.

The river, now frozen, a glistening span,
Reflects all the dreams of a world that began.
With warmth in our hearts and the chill in the air,
We cherish the moments, so precious and rare.

Winter's soft touch paints the landscape anew,
In each snowy flake, a world to pursue.
There's magic in stillness, in every cold breath,
A moment of peace that defies even death.

So let us embrace this enchanting display,
Where nature's pure beauty finds space to play.
For in every season, there's a rhythm and grace,
In Nature's soft whispers, our worries erase.

The Stillness of December's Breath

In December's hush, a calmness unfolds,
The air crisp and clear, whispers secrets untold.
Each breath forms a cloud, a soft, fleeting dream,
As daylight slips softly, like a gentle stream.

Frosted windows frame the world out of sight,
While crackling fires dance with warmth and delight.
Candles flicker softly, casting shadows so thin,
A cozy reminder of the warmth found within.

The moon hangs so high, bright in the night,
Illuminating paths with its silvery light.
Every snow-laden branch bows low to the ground,
As nature breathes softly, a symphony found.

The stillness of night wraps the world up so tight,
Cradled in peace, lost in quiet delight.
Each moment a treasure as time softly slows,
In December's embrace, where serenity glows.

Embrace the still whispers of nights that are cold,
The stories of winter, in memories told.
With each heartfelt sigh, let the wonders unfold,
For magic is woven in the stillness of gold.

A Glacial Glisten

Icicles dangle like fragile glass beams,
Reflecting the sunlight with sparkling gleams.
In silence they hang, like jewels from the sky,
Whispering tales as they catch the eye.

The river flows slow, a shimmering belt,
Under the frost, the winter is felt.
A canvas of white, where the wild creatures tread,
Sealed in the magic that winter has spread.

With each step we take on the crisp powdered ground,
The crunch of the snow is a soft, soothing sound.
A world dressed in crystals, a sight to behold,
As nature unveils her purest of gold.

The sun in its glory, a warming embrace,
Melts briefly the chill from this beautiful place.
For in every corner, there's wonder to find,
In the glacial glisten, our hearts are aligned.

So let us rejoice in this beauty so rare,
With laughter and joy, we break free from despair.
The magic of winter, in its soft, fleeting grace,
Creates a connection we all can embrace.

Pinecones Cloaked in Frost

Pinecones adorned with a frosty white lace,
Nestled in branches, a delicate place.
Nature's small treasures, so quiet, so shy,
Bathe in the glow of the crisp winter sky.

The scent of the pine, rich in the cold air,
Whispers secrets of seasons, a story we share.
Beneath the vast sky where the snowflakes fall,
These sturdy reminders stand bravely through all.

The crunch of the frost spills beneath our feet,
Each step a sweet echo, a heartwarming beat.
Rustling leaves tell of the life that remains,
In the depths of the winter, the spirit sustains.

Each pinecone a promise, a future untold,
Of growth in the spring when the world turns to gold.
In the heart of the pines, a beautiful sight,
A cycle of life in the soft morning light.

So cherish the stillness, the beauty that binds,
In nature's grand tapestry where heart loves and finds.
For even in winter, with its chill and its cost,
There's magic in pinecones, forever embossed.

The Stillness After the Storm

The clouds drift off, a soft goodbye,
Leaves swirl gently, the wind sighs.
Puddles sparkle, reflecting light,
Birds return, ready to take flight.

The air is fresh, the world made new,
A quiet calm, in every hue.
Sunbeams break through the grayish veil,
A whispered promise, a soothing tale.

Flowers peek from the damp, dark earth,
Each petal gleams, a sign of rebirth.
Nature breathes, an easy pause,
In this stillness, our hearts applause.

Time at rest, as if to dream,
Life resumes with a gentle gleam.
Moments linger, sweet and bright,
In the hush of the fading light.

So let us savor this peaceful hour,
A chance to bloom, to grow, to flower.
For after storms, we truly see,
The beauty found in harmony.

Nature's Frosted Palate

Whispers of winter, soft and light,
Blankets of white, pure delight.
Each branch adorned, a crystal lace,
Nature's art, a stunning grace.

The frosty air, a brisk embrace,
Chill in the wind, a gentle trace.
Footprints mark the path we tread,
In this wonderland, softly spread.

Icicles dangle from rooftops high,
Like nature's jewels that catch the eye.
Silence blankets the sleeping trees,
As the world holds its breath with ease.

Birds in the distance, their song so clear,
Echoes in time, a melody dear.
Nature's buffet, each color so bold,
Rich in flavors, a sight to behold.

Take in the beauty, let it unfold,
In the stillness, our hearts are consoled.
For in this frost, there's warmth to be found,
In nature's embrace, we are deeply bound.

The December Veil in Twilight

As daylight fades, a veil descends,
Soft shadows stretch, the daylight ends.
Stars awaken in the dusky sky,
Whispers of night begin to fly.

The air is crisp, the quiet deep,
In this twilight hour, secrets keep.
Moonlight bathes the earth in glow,
A silver river, serene and slow.

Frost-kissed grass, a shimmering sheet,
Underfoot, it makes a gentle beat.
The world transforms with each passing hue,
Colors blend in a palette anew.

Trees stand tall, their branches sway,
As night unfolds, they softly play.
Nature sleeps, a tranquil rest,
In the twilight, we are blessed.

Breathe in the peace, let worries cease,
For in this moment, we find release.
The December veil embraces all,
In its whisper, we hear the call.

Sighing Branches Under the Weight

Branches bow low, heavy with snow,
Whispers of winter in breezes flow.
Beneath the burden, they softly sigh,
As flakes cascade from the gray, dim sky.

Each limb a story, each leaf a dream,
In the chill of hush, the world does seem.
A moment captured in time's embrace,
Nature's patience holds a tender space.

The forest breathes in quiet tones,
Underneath the weight, life's heart still moans.
Crimson berries, a splash of cheer,
Amidst the white, their colors appear.

As twilight lingers, shadows grow long,
Nature hums a soft, soothing song.
With every sigh, the earth finds grace,
Under the weight, a calming place.

In the stillness, find a path to roam,
Sighing branches lead us home.
For in their bending, wisdom we find,
Resilience blooms in nature's kind.

Quietude of the Pines

In the stillness, shadows play,
Beneath the boughs, a soft ballet.
Whispers of secrets in rustling leaves,
Nature's calm, as the heart believes.

Moonlight drapes a silver sheen,
Pine trees stand in shades of green.
Echoes of night, the silence calls,
Mysteries linger, as twilight falls.

Footsteps tread on soft, cool ground,
In this haven, peace is found.
Stars emerge, a diamond crown,
In the quietude, no need to drown.

Breath of earth, a soothing sigh,
Swaying branches in the sky.
Harmony weaves through every strand,
In the pines, we understand.

Rest in this tranquil embrace,
Nature offers a gentle space.
Amongst the trees, lost in time,
The heart finds rhythm, soft and prime.

A Diary in Ice

Pages of frost under moon's glow,
Whispers of winter in each shadow.
Silent storms in a frozen frame,
Nature's ink, in crystal, it came.

Footprints etched on the icy scene,
Stories written, serene and keen.
Breezes carry the tales of old,
In the chill, every memory told.

Branches heavy with frosty lace,
Winter's touch in this silent place.
A diary closed, secrets kept,
In the cold, nature has wept.

Time stands still in this frozen prose,
Each breath exhaled, a vapor flows.
Under the stars, the world asleep,
In icy silence, promises keep.

Moments captured in winter's embrace,
A diary filled with hope and grace.
Nature reflects its poignant art,
In ice and snow, a frozen heart.

The Essence of Chilled Air

A breath of frost, the morning wakes,
Soft whispers dance on the lakes.
In every corner, the coolness spreads,
Kissing the earth where life treads.

Transparent clouds in a sunlit sky,
Echoes of frost as the chill floats by.
Each inhalation, crisp and clear,
Draws the essence of winter near.

Branches adorned with ice's art,
Nature's palette, a wondrous part.
In the gentle hush of the cool air,
Moments linger, suspended, rare.

Evening descends with a silken veil,
Chilled air wraps like a soft tale.
In the twilight, the essence glows,
A whispering magic that winter knows.

Breath by breath, we gauge the time,
In chilled air, we find the rhyme.
Fusion of seasons, a dance so fair,
In the essence of winter's air.

Whispers of Winter's Breath

A gentle hush in the frosty night,
Whispers travel, soft and light.
Snowflakes flutter with teasing grace,
Winter's breath in a soft embrace.

Ghostly murmurs in the pines,
Each chill note, a secret shines.
Echoes linger in the moon's embrace,
Stories told in this silent space.

Frosty patterns on windowpanes,
Whispers carried like soft refrains.
Nature sings under a starry sheet,
Every pulse, a rhythmic beat.

Icicles glint like silver threads,
In the stillness, magic spreads.
As shadows stretch, the night endears,
Winter's breath melts all our fears.

In every breeze, a tale is spun,
Whispers of winter, a soft run.
Each moment savored, a gentle caress,
In the warmth of dreams, we find our rest.

A Tapestry of Icy Gemstones

Glistening crystals catch the light,
A tapestry of blue and white.
Hues of nature, pure delight,
Sparkling gems, a wondrous sight.

Whispers dance in the frigid air,
Each flake delicate, beyond compare.
Woven softly through the trees,
A cloak of winter's gentle breeze.

Frozen echoes fill the night,
Moonlit gems, a soft invite.
In their beauty, silence gleams,
Beneath the stars, we find our dreams.

Every corner, every edge,
Nature's artistry, a pledge.
An icy shimmer, pure and bright,
Captures hearts in winter's light.

In this stillness, time stands still,
Breath of cold, a tranquil thrill.
A tapestry, nature's grace,
In icy gemstones we find our place.

Pine Sighs in Winter Light

Pine trees whisper in the frost,
Secrets of the seasons lost.
Beneath their boughs, the silence grows,
In winter light, a still repose.

Softly falling, flakes descend,
Nature's quilt, a soft blend.
Golden sun on needles bright,
Glimmers softly, pure delight.

Echoes linger in the chill,
Every breath, a silver thrill.
Pine sighs tell of tales untold,
Cradling warmth against the cold.

Crisp and fragrant, fresh and low,
A quiet path where dreams can flow.
In the stillness, time does pause,
Winter's beauty earns applause.

Underneath the starry veil,
In the night, the quiet pale.
With every breath, a whispered song,
Pine sighs in winter light belong.

Echoes of Stillness and Cold

Echoes ripple through the trees,
Whispers caught in frosty breeze.
Every shadow, every sound,
Holds the stillness all around.

Underneath a moonlit glow,
Silent paths where soft winds blow.
In the quiet, time extends,
Embracing all that winter sends.

Frozen branches, crystal lace,
Nature's breath, a gentle grace.
In the hush, we find the peace,
Where worries fade and sighs decrease.

In the air, a frosty tale,
Bringing whispers through the vale.
Echoes dance on icy ground,
In stillness, warmth is found.

Each moment, wrapped in white,
Tender shadows, soft and light.
Nature's song of cold and calm,
In the silence, life's sweet balm.

Twilight's Embrace on Needles

Twilight falls on needles fine,
Dancing shadows intertwine.
In gentle hues, the world transforms,
Wrapped in soft, embracing forms.

The air hangs thick with fragrant pine,
Whispers of the dusk define.
As daylight fades, the stars awake,
In twilight's grasp, the heart will ache.

Needles glisten, bathed in gold,
Stories of the night unfold.
Each moment savored, soft and sweet,
In twilight's embrace, all is complete.

A canvas painted with the dusk,
Life's quiet rhythms in soft husk.
Stars emerge with gentle might,
In shadows deep, they share their light.

The world a dream in twilight's hue,
Softening edges, calming blue.
As night descends, we find our place,
In twilight's arms, we bask in grace.

A Breath of Ice Over the Forest

Whispers dance upon the air,
Chill descends with quiet grace.
Branches bow, a frosted flair,
Nature's breath leaves a soft trace.

Glistening crystals catch the light,
Each leaf dons a sparkling cloak.
Silent beauty, pure and bright,
In the stillness, dreams evoke.

Footprints crunch on snowflakes deep,
A chilly wind begins to weave.
Secrets of the woods to keep,
In this frozen, quiet reprieve.

Overhead, the gray clouds loom,
Yet within, a warmth prevails.
In nature's heart, the silent bloom,
As winter's breath tells its tales.

A moment frozen, time stands still,
Underneath the snowy skies.
Each breath a gift, pure winter's chill,
Echoing in the forest sighs.

Frigid Beauty in Nature's Heart

Amidst the pines, the frost does cling,
Beauty framed in icy lace.
Softly, nature starts to sing,
Melodies of time and space.

Winter's hush brings calm and peace,
Every flake a work of art.
In this season, worries cease,
Serenity, a tender heart.

Crisp air carries scents of pine,
A fleeting touch, a fleeting sound.
In this wonder, we align,
With nature's grace, our souls are bound.

Breezes whisper through the trees,
As shadows dance upon the ground.
Winter's breath, a gentle tease,
In the quiet, love is found.

With every step, the world awakes,
Transformed by icy, silken threads.
Around us, nature softly shakes,
In this chill, our spirit treads.

The Frosted Wreath of Branches

Upon the trees, a wreath of white,
Frosted branches sway and bend.
Amidst the cold, a pure delight,
Nature's magic, hearts to mend.

Every bough, adorned with grace,
Each flake a gentle, silent kiss.
In this pause, we find our place,
In winter's cold, we find our bliss.

Hushed whispers float on frosty air,
A realm of glimmering dreams abound.
In these woods, our souls laid bare,
As peace envelops all around.

Steps muffled in a snowy quilt,
Where hearts unite in frosted space.
In this realm, all worries wilt,
Wrapped in winter's soft embrace.

Through the trees, the sun peeks bright,
Casting rays on frosted ground.
While day unfolds, it feels so right,
In this moment, love is found.

Echoes of Crystal-Kissed Pines

In the stillness, echoes ring,
Crystal-kissed the pines stand tall.
Whispers of the winter sing,
In this fortress, nature's call.

With branches draped in frozen sheen,
The world transforms beneath the light.
A tapestry, serene and keen,
Guiding souls through winter's night.

Beneath the sky, a canvas gray,
Each wind-blown flake, a fleeting guest.
Carving paths in a gentle way,
Embracing all, giving rest.

In the depth, a warmth persists,
Within this chill, our spirits rise.
Through the frosty mist, we exist,
Mirrored in the winter skies.

As shadows stretch and daylight wanes,
Frosted beauty softly glows.
In each breath, the stillness reigns,
In nature's hold, the heart knows.

Pine Needles Wrapped in White

Pine needles cloaked in a blanket of snow,
Silence unfolds where the cold winds blow.
Branches bow down, heavy with dreams,
Nature whispers softly, or so it seems.

Footprints vanish on the glittering ground,
Every step echoes, a hushed, gentle sound.
The sun peeks shyly through frosted boughs,
Awakening beauty, honoring vows.

Icicles glisten like stars in the night,
Mirroring hope with a delicate light.
Laced in silver, the world stands still,
Wrapped in a magic that time cannot kill.

Every breath leaves a cloud in the air,
A fleeting moment, a silence to share.
In this winter's embrace, I find my peace,
A landscape of wonder, where worries cease.

So let the cold come, let the winds sing,
Embrace the season that winter can bring.
For in these pine needles wrapped in white,
I discover the beauty in each frosted sight.

The Elegance of Winter's Garb

A delicate dance in the whispers of cold,
Winter's garb woven from stories untold.
Each flake a promise, unique in its form,
Blanketing earth with a crystalline charm.

Trees wear their coats, elegantly white,
While shadows stretch long in the fading light.
Silhouettes glimmer, each curve and each line,
Stitched by the frost and the hands of divine.

Crisp air awakens the senses anew,
A refreshing breath of a tranquil blue.
The world is a canvas where dreams softly flow,
The elegance whispers in pathways of snow.

Beneath the cold sky, stars start to gleam,
Life pauses sweetly, caught in a dream.
In the stillness, I find strength to embrace,
The beauty of winter, its timeless grace.

Let moments linger like prints in the snow,
Each brush of the chill, a soft, loving glow.
In winter's embrace, my heart learns to sing,
In the elegance of this season's offering.

Dreamlike Landscapes of Frost

In the hush of dawn, frost paints the scene,
Creating a world where magic's routine.
Fields dipped in silver, a shimmering sight,
Dreamlike landscapes wake with soft morning light.

The breath of the earth, a soft, gentle sigh,
As icicles dangle from branches up high.
Nature's artwork sprawled, untouched and serene,
A world crafted tenderly, calm and pristine.

Footsteps I leave, a trail in the white,
Stories unfold in the crispness of night.
Stars overhead twinkle, as if to agree,
That in this still moment, a dreamer is free.

The rivers freeze swiftly, veiled in a cloak,
Whispers of winter dance softly like smoke.
Soft whispers allure, as the shadows convene,
In dreamlike landscapes, where moments are seen.

So let me wander, where the frost softly glows,
In this canvas of wonder, my spirit bestows.
For here in the silence, I find what I seek,
In the beauty of winter, my heart learns to speak.

Gliding Through a Winter Wonderland

Snowflakes are falling, a magical sight,
Dancing on air, pure enchantment in flight.
Glistening trails weave through evergreen trees,
Nature transformed by a soft, gentle breeze.

Children are laughing, their joy fills the air,
Sleds race downhill, without any care.
With cheeks rosy red, they cherish this bliss,
Each moment a treasure, none wanting to miss.

The crunch of the snow 'neath the boots of the brave,
Leads to adventures down valleys and caves.
Gliding through wonder, a realm made of dreams,
Where laughter and joy are the heart's vibrant themes.

As twilight approaches, the sky turns to gold,
Fires crackle warmly, a story unfolds.
Families gather, with hearts open wide,
In this winter wonderland, love cannot hide.

Starry nights settle as whispers exchange,
Memories crafted, as seasons arrange.
So here I will linger, with spirits unplanned,
Forever embracing this winter wonderland.

Milton Keynes UK
Ingram Content Group UK Ltd.
UKHW010228111224
452348UK00011B/588